Kick, Hit, Bowl!

by Rachel Russ

OXFORD
UNIVERSITY PRESS

Look at all the balls.

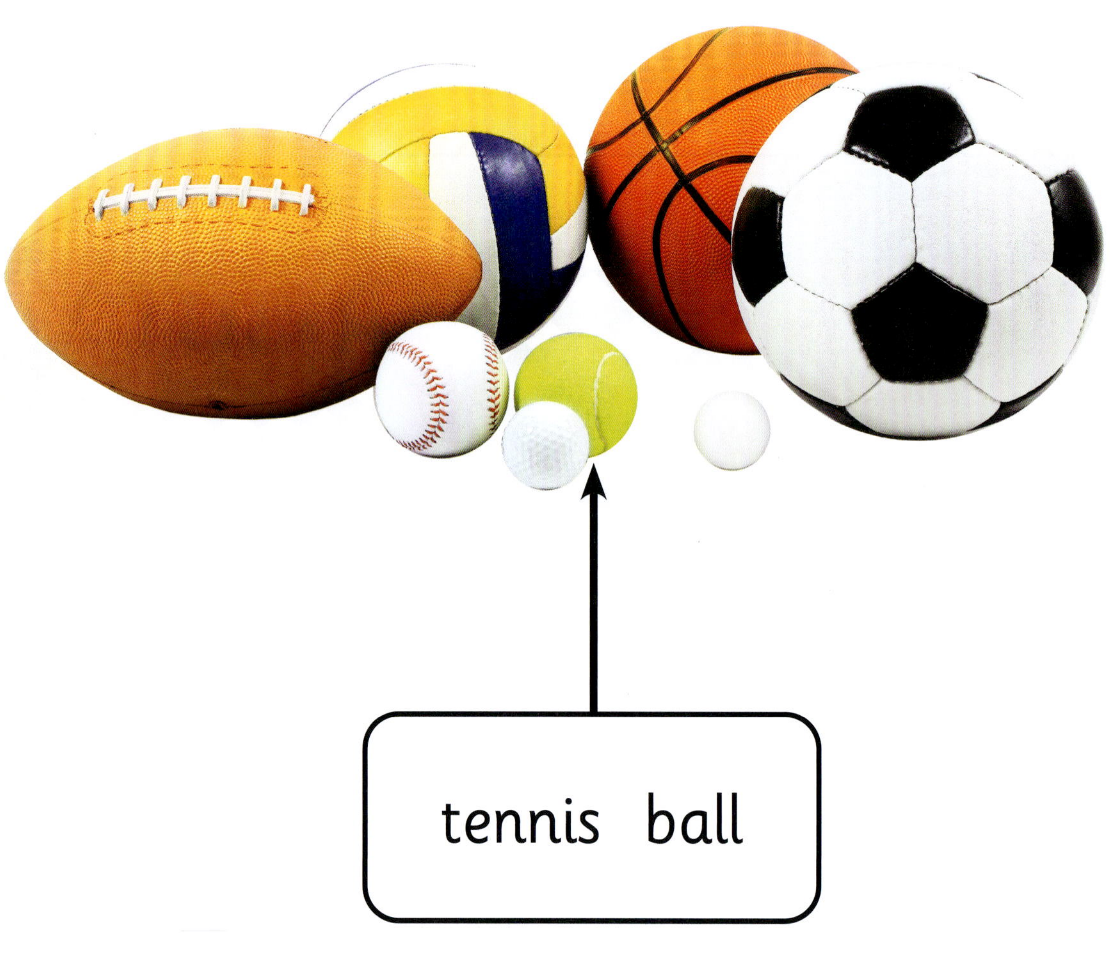

We can kick them.

We can hit them and bowl them.

Kick it!

Can you kick the ball into the goal?

You kick this ball, too!

You hit the tennis ball.

Hit it low or high!

Hit it higher than the net.

A bowler tosses this ball.

A batter hits it.

She secures her pads.

This ball is quick.

Hit it with the bat.

Bowl it!

Toss the big ball.

Be sure to hit the pins.

Bowl this ball.

Get it near the jack.

Shoot for it!

Shoot this ball into the tall hoop.

You shoot this ball, too.

She shoots it into the net.

Bowl the ball.

Kick the ball.

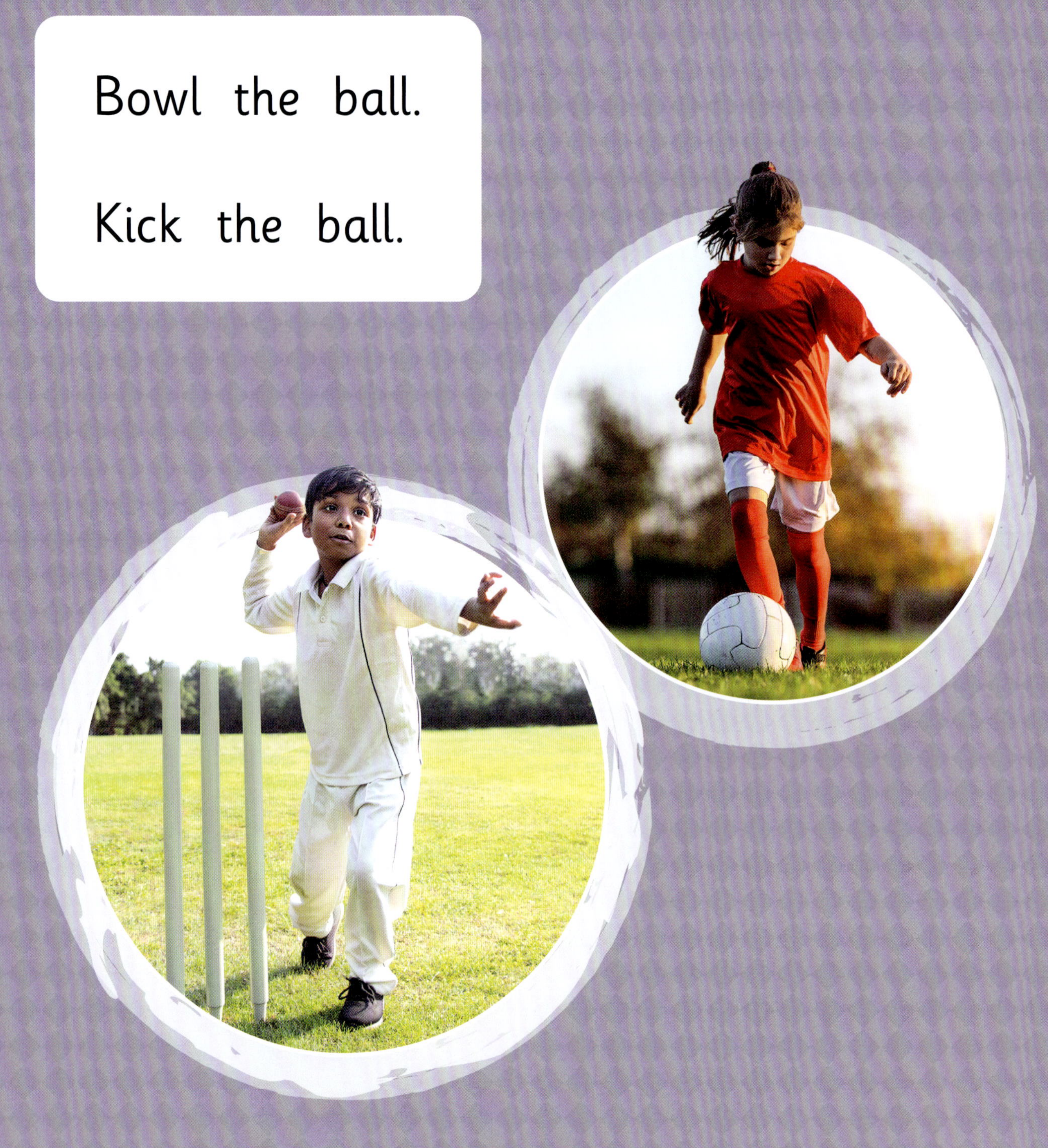

Hit the ball.

Shoot the ball.

Look Back

Encourage students to use the images to review the topic.